Playful

There are dozens of dog breeds to choose from: Labrador retriever, chihuahua, miniature dachshund, beagle, pug and more.

Cute

Using the wireless Bark mode, your pup can search for doggy playmates, and will start barking if another Nintendogs owner is nearby.

Active

Your Nintendog is an ultrarealistic puppy to play with and care for. Just like the real thing, your puppy responds to your voice and touch.

Table of Contents

Puppy Breeds

A complete listing of all 20 breeds.

Lyndon B. Johnson owned three beagles named Him, Her and Edgar.

BEAGLE

FACTS

Origin:	Great Britain
Height:	33-41cm
Weight:	8-14kg

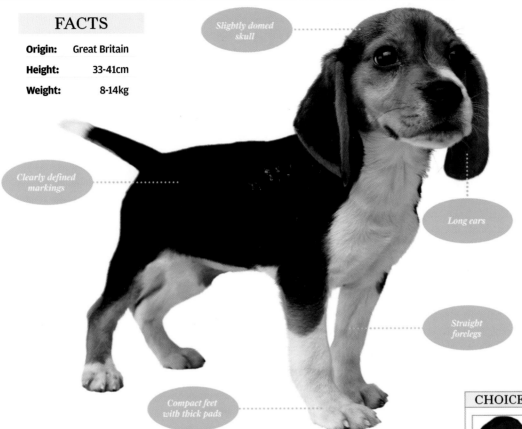

Slightly domed skull

Clearly defined markings

Long ears

Straight forelegs

Compact feet with thick pads

 ## *Happiness is a warm beagle*

Curiosity may have killed the cat, but it's helped the beagle become one of the most popular dogs in the world. Its inquisitive nature and incredible sense of smell have made the beagle a longtime favorite among hunters, police and even the British royal family, whose members were so fond of beagles they would often carry them around in small satchels (some smaller breeds are still called "pocket beagles"). The beagle's playful personality and love of children makes it a natural choice for kids, but this hyperactive hound can be high-maintenance—lack of exercise and a poor diet can turn your regal beagle into a roly-poly!

CHOICES

This is a starting breed in the Dachshund & Friends and Dalmatian & Friends versions. You can trade for it or unlock it in other Nintendogs versions.

The Boxer was one of the first breeds selected in Germany for police training.

BOXER

FACTS

Origin:	Germany
Height:	53-63 cm
Weight:	25-32 kg

Mask confined to muzzle

Strong, muscular neck without dewlap

Short, straight muscular back

Well-arched ribs

Strong, straight, firmly muscled forelegs

CHOICES

This is a starting breed in the Chihuahua & Friends and Dalmatian & Friends versions. You can trade for it or unlock it in other Nintendogs versions.

He's a lover, not a fighter

Despite its pugnacious appearance, the boxer is a lovable clown with a penchant for comic mischief. This fun-loving breed has several boxer-specific ways of amusing its owners, including "kidney beaning," a spinning dance the dog does when it's excited. Another memorable trait of the boxer is the "woo-woo" sound it makes when it wants to get your attention. Though originally bred for hunting, the modern boxer would rather snuggle in your lap than chase prey.

CAVALIER KING CHARLES SPANIEL

The King Charles was featured on the hit television series Sex and the City *as Charlotte York's dog.*

Relatively flat, undomed skull

Long, silky coat with no curls

Long, well-feathered ears

FACTS

Origin:	Great Britain
Height:	31-33 cm
Weight:	5-8 kg

The dog who would be king

The Cavalier is a direct descendant of the toy spaniels seen in paintings of kings and queens during the 17th century. Today's cavalier King Charles, however, is more likely to be seen catching a disc in the park than lounging in a palace. Dog toys aren't the only thing the breed likes to pursue, though—the fearless spaniel will chase after cars if left unattended, so be sure to keep this lovable leaper on a short leash.

CHOICES

This is a starting breed in the Chihuahua & Friends version. You can trade for it or unlock it in other Nintendogs versions.

CHIHUAHUA

Pictures of dogs resembling the modern Chihuahua appear in ancient paintings in Mexico.

FACTS

Origin:	Mexico
Height:	15-23 cm
Weight:	1-3 kg

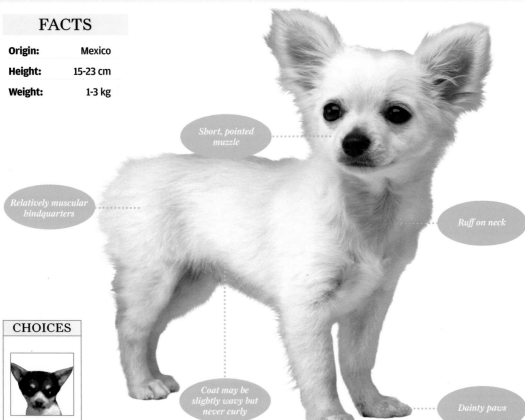

Short, pointed muzzle

Relatively muscular hindquarters

Ruff on neck

Coat may be slightly wavy but never curly

Dainty paws

CHOICES

This is a starting breed in the Chihuahua & Friends version. You can trade for it or unlock it in other Nintendogs versions.

All that shivers is gold

You'd never guess by looking at it, but the Chihuahua's ancestors were worshiped by the ancient Aztecs. This shivering, pint-sized pup is a direct descendant of the Techichi dogs that were sacred icons used as spirit guides to the dead. Despite its diminutive stature (it's the smallest breed registered with the American Kennel Club), the Chihuahua can be fiercely protective of its owner, and has been known to take on much larger dogs or even people if it feels threatened.

George Washington, Benjamin Franklin and Pablo Picasso all owned dalmations.

DALMATIAN

FACTS

Origin: Eastern Europe

Height: 56-61 cm

Weight: 23-25 kg

Ears are set high on head and taper to a round point

Round hindquarters

Short, hard, dense hair

Straight forelegs

Round, well-arched, catlike feet

CHOICES

This is a starting breed in the Dalmatian & Friends version. You can trade for in or unlock it in other Nintendogs versions.

 ## *A firefighter's best friend*

Over the years, dalmations have worked as retrievers, guard dogs and circus performers, but this polka-dotted pooch will forever be known as a fire dog. In the 1800s, American firefighters started using dalmations to control the horses that pulled the fire engines. They were also used to guard the fire equipment from rival fire departments, who would try to sabotage each other to get to the fires first. Even though the days of horse-drawn fire engines and cutthroat firefighters are long gone, the dalmatian remains the trusted mascot of fire stations across America.

GERMAN SHEPHERD DOG

The German shepherd dog has been in the public eye many times, thanks to Rin Tin Tin and other canine characters.

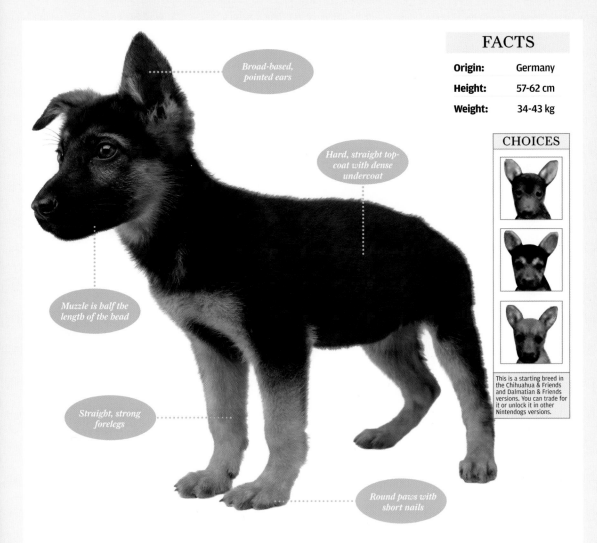

FACTS

Origin:	Germany
Height:	57-62 cm
Weight:	34-43 kg

Broad-based, pointed ears

Hard, straight top-coat with dense undercoat

Muzzle is half the length of the head

Straight, strong forelegs

Round paws with short nails

CHOICES

This is a starting breed in the Chihuahua & Friends and Dalmatian & Friends versions. You can trade for it or unlock it in other Nintendogs versions.

A pup of all trades

A versatile and enthusiastic worker, the German shepherd dog ranks among the most popular breeds in the world. The highly intelligent shepherd dog has served in many capacities over the years, including messenger, watchdog, rescue worker and guide dog (Helen Keller's was a German shepherd). Although by nature they are wary of strangers, once you befriend a German shepherd dog he will be a trusted companion for life.

Golden retrievers excel at hunting, obedience, and field trials, and are superb guide dogs.

GOLDEN RETRIEVER

FACTS

Origin:	Great Britain
Height:	51-61 cm
Weight:	27-36 kg

CHOICES

This is a starting breed in the Dachshund & Friends and Dalmatian & Friends versions. You can trade for it or unlock it in other Nintendogs versions.

Broad skull and powerful muzzle

Ears level with eyes

Wavy or flat coat

Straight, well-boned forelegs

Round, catlike paws

 ## *Blondes have more fun*

K nown as a "bird dog," the golden retriever was originally bred in the British Isles to fetch fallen quail and ducks for hunters. The modern-day retriever still has this hunting instinct, although he usually uses it to fetch sticks or tennis balls. Loving and affectionate with children, the golden retriever is one of the most family-friendly dogs around. This well-mannered, easy-to-train breed can be taught to perform almost any canine job except guard dog—he's far too lovable to pose a threat (although he *could* pounce on intruders and lick them into submission).

The breed got its name from renowned British huntsman Reverend John (Jack) Russell, who had a great passion for fox hunting, hounds and working terriers.

JACK RUSSELL TERRIER

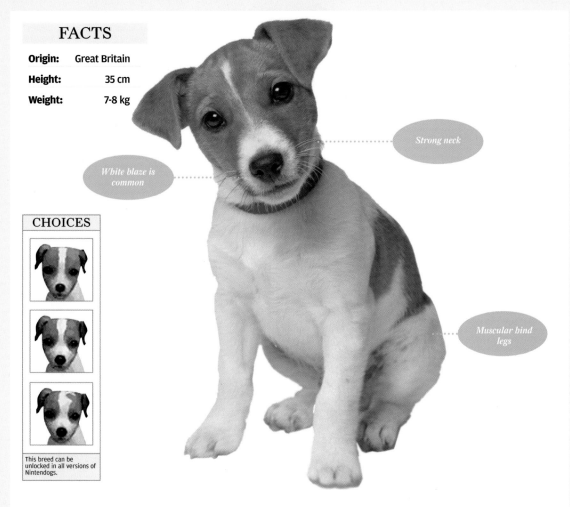

FACTS

Origin:	Great Britain
Height:	35 cm
Weight:	7-8 kg

Strong neck

White blaze is common

Muscular hind legs

CHOICES

This breed can be unlocked in all versions of Nintendogs.

 ## Jack be nimble, Jack be quick

The athletic, energetic Jack Russell terrier was originally bred to use its keen sense of smell to help hunters track down foxes. Its insatiable sniffer, however, can lead this curious canine into serious mischief chasing down squirrels, birds or even cars. The dog loves to get dirty, and you might spend hours trying to get this pup clean after a day of digging in the backyard. With constant supervision and proper obedience training, though, the good-natured Jack Russell terrier can be a loving and entertaining pet pal.

The pedigrees of two of the most influential Labs, Peter of Faskally and Flapper, go back as far as 1878.

LABRADOR RETRIEVER

FACTS

Origin:	Canada
Height:	54-57 cm
Weight:	25-34 kg

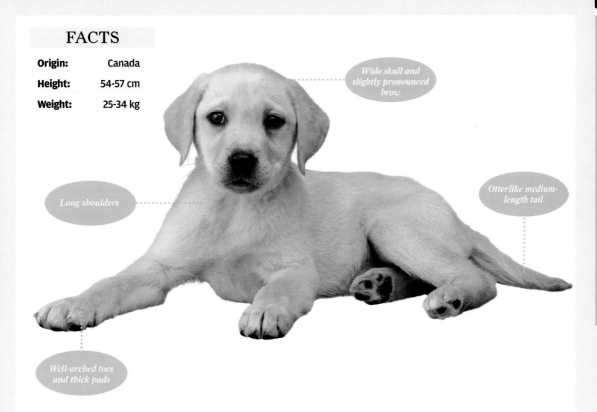

Wide skull and slightly pronounced brow

Otterlike medium-length tail

Long shoulders

Well-arched toes and thick pads

CHOICES

This is a starting breed in the Lab & Friends version. You can trade for it or unlock it in other Nintendogs versions.

 ## *The Labrador lifeguard*

Hailing from Newfoundland, Canada, the Labrador retriever was once used by fishermen to jump overboard into the icy water and haul in their nets. It's no wonder the modern Labrador retriever's favorite pastime is to play in the water. Unlike most breeds, which mature into adulthood after only a year, the Lab is considered a puppy for the first three years of its life, which may explain its playful nature. Besides being a fun-loving family dog, Labradors often act as guide dogs, and have even been trained to detect drugs and explosives.

Miniature dachshunds are accomplished hunting dogs despite their lapdog reputation.

FACTS

Origin:	Germany
Height:	13-23 cm
Weight:	4-5 kg

Wide mouth opening behind level of eyes

Coat longest on neck and underparts

Hind feet smaller than forefeet

CHOICES

This is a starting breed in the Dachshund & Friends version. You can trade for it or unlock it in other Nintendogs versions.

This hotdog can hunt

Don't let his comical looks fool you—the sausage-shaped miniature dachshund (commonly referred to as a "wiener dog") can be a fierce fighter. Over 100 years ago, miniature dachshunds were bred specifically to hunt badgers (dachshund means "badger dog" in German). The miniature dachshund's tubelike body is perfect for chasing badgers into their long, skinny underground burrows, and the dachshund is the only AKC-recognized breed that hunts both above and below ground. Although it is rarely used for hunting any more, the fearless miniature dachshund has been known to destroy unsuspecting squeak toys with its powerful jaws.

The "min pin," as it is called among fanciers, is noted for its intelligence and pep.

MINIATURE PINSCHER

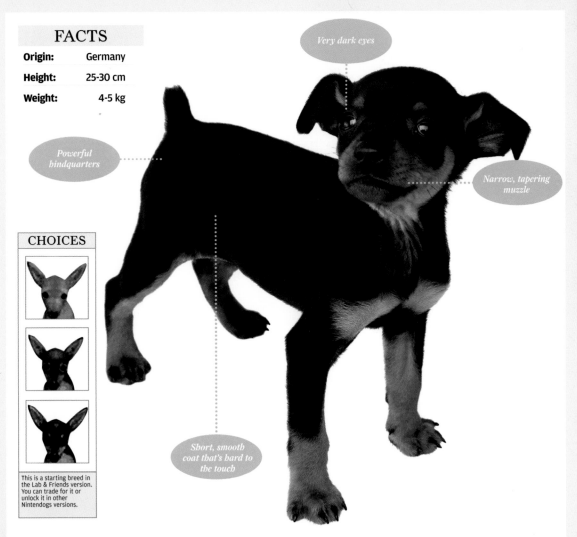

FACTS

Origin:	Germany
Height:	25-30 cm
Weight:	4-5 kg

Very dark eyes

Powerful hindquarters

Narrow, tapering muzzle

Short, smooth coat that's hard to the touch

CHOICES

This is a starting breed in the Lab & Friends version. You can trade for it or unlock it in other Nintendogs versions.

🐾 *The king of toys*

The miniature pinscher, often referred to as the "king of toys," is listed in the "toy" group by the American Kennel Club, but this powerful pup is no helpless plaything. Although he is not directly related to the giant Doberman pinscher, the miniature pinscher seems to think he's as big as one, ready to defend his home and owner against any suspicious strangers. This supersmall-fry is a bundle of energy, so you'll get plenty of exercise if you invite him into your home.

Senators Bob and Elizabeth Dole, actor Bill Cosby, and actor/martial artist Bruce Lee have all owned miniature schnauzers.

MINIATURE SCHNAUZER

V-shaped ears, high on head, hanging forward

Prominent black nose and wide nostrils

Forelegs appear straight from every angle

FACTS

Origin:	Germany
Height:	33-36 cm
Weight:	6-7 kg

CHOICES

This is a starting breed in and Lab & Friends version. You can trade for it or unlock it in other Nintendogs versions.

 ## Little big dog

The miniature schnauzer may be small, but it's not weak or fragile. In fact, if you were to pick up a miniature schnauzer, you'd discover he's sturdy and muscular—a really pumped-up pup! Originally bred as a farm dog, the miniature schnauzer is a great house pet and is known to become very attached to its owners—so attached, in fact, that owners may have a hard time keeping him out of their bed at night. Since he's built so low to the ground, the miniature schnauzer excels at catching rodents (and occasionally an owner's slippers).

The Pembroke Welsh corgi, unlike the Cardigan, has almost no tail.

PEMBROKE WELSH CORGI

FACTS

Origin:	Great Britain
Height:	25-31 cm
Weight:	10-12.5 kg

Pricked, medium-size ears

Slightly tapering muzzle

Short tail and strong bindquarters

Powerful neck

CHOICES

This is a starting breed in the Lab & Friends version. You can trade for it or unlock it in other Nintendogs versions.

The Welsh wonderdog

Legend says the Pembroke Welsh corgi is an enchanted dog, used by fairies and elves to pull carriages and work the fields for the wee folk. If you look closely, you may even spot the marks of a "fairy saddle" on the corgi's shoulder fur. The breed originated in Pembrokeshire, Wales, and was used mostly for herding cattle. The modern Welsh corgi still possesses the urge to herd, and will sometimes try to herd its human family members by nipping at their heels. In recent years, the Pembroke Welsh corgi has become internationally known as the favorite pet of Queen Elizabeth II.

The pug was a pet of the Buddhist monasteries in Tibet.

PUG

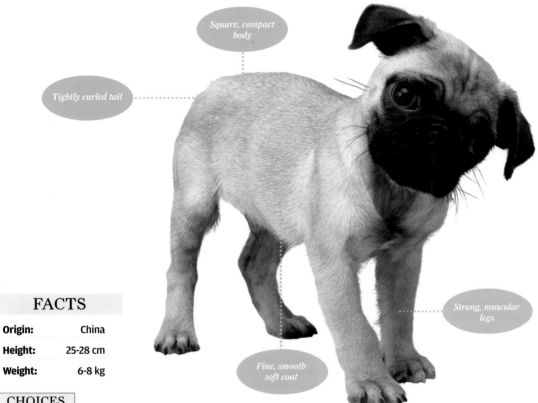

Square, compact body

Tightly curled tail

Strong, muscular legs

Fine, smooth soft coat

FACTS

Origin:	China
Height:	25-28 cm
Weight:	6-8 kg

CHOICES

This is a starting breed in the Dachshund & Friends version. You can trade for it or unlock it in other Nintendogs versions.

 International dog of mystery

F ew dogs have witnessed as many historical events as the pug. This mysterious Asian breed is believed to have originated in China sometime before 400 BC. They were prized possessions of the emperors of China and at times were even guarded by soldiers. In 1572, a pug saved the life of the young prince of Holland. In the 1800s, Napoleon's wife Josephine sent secret messages to her husband under the collar of her pug. The squarely and solidly built pug remains popular today, and even landed a role as an alien in the 1997 film *Men in Black*.

Also known as the sheltie, the Shetland sheepdog is one of the most successful obedience breeds.

SHETLAND SHEEPDOG

Small ears set close together

Level back

Distinctive mane

Feathering on back of forelegs

FACTS

Origin:	Great Britain
Height:	35-37 cm
Weight:	6-7 kg

CHOICES

This is a starting breed in the Chihuahua & Friends version. You can trade for it or unlock it in other Nintendogs versions.

 ## The sheepmaster

Although Shetland sheepdogs look like pint-sized Lassies, they are not miniature collies. They are, in fact, a completely different breed, but they do share a common profession: sheep herding. Shetland sheepdogs are some of the best herding dogs in the world, and even urban shelties have a hard time fighting the urge to round up and protect a herd. Their loud, distinct bark keeps strangers at bay, and their gentle nature and high intelligence make them ideal family pets.

Shibas are among the smallest of the Japanese breeds, and are thought to be the oldest.

SHIBA INU

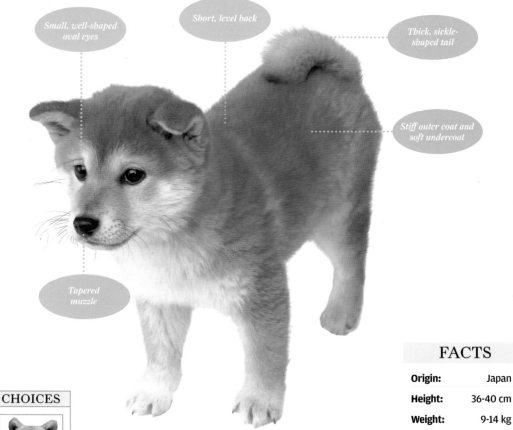

Small, well-shaped oval eyes

Short, level back

Thick, sickle-shaped tail

Stiff outer coat and soft undercoat

Tapered muzzle

FACTS

Origin:	Japan
Height:	36-40 cm
Weight:	9-14 kg

CHOICES

This is a starting breed in the Lab & Friends version. You can trade for it or unlock it in other Nintendogs versions.

🐾 *Little wolf, big bite*

Nicknamed "little wolf," the shiba inu is one of the most commonly kept dogs in Japan. Despite its cute and cuddly appearance, the shiba inu has been used as a guard dog for centuries. This wee watchdog was even used to hunt wild boar in the dense highland forests of its native country. The origins of the breed go back more than 2,000 years—images of the dog have been found in ancient scrolls, paintings and carvings.

The shih tzu was the house pet for most of the Ming dynasty.

SHIH TZU

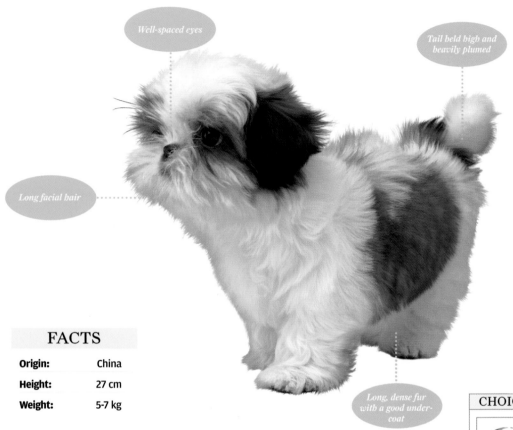

Well-spaced eyes

Tail held high and heavily plumed

Long facial hair

Long, dense fur with a good under-coat

FACTS

Origin:	China
Height:	27 cm
Weight:	5-7 kg

A lap-sized lion

With the mane of a lion and a face like a Danish, the tiny shih tzu is easy to fall in love with. Originally bred in the Forbidden City of Peking in the 16th century, the shih tzu was held in such high regard by the Chinese imperial court that they refused to trade or sell it to the West until 1930. An alert little watchdog, the shih tzu likes to bark but is usually quiet and well-behaved, and makes an excellent indoor companion.

CHOICES

This is a starting breed in the Dachshund & Friends version. You can trade for it or unlock it in other Nintendogs versions.

In 1925, the city of Nome, Alaska, was stricken by a diphtheria epidemic, and dog teams of Siberians led heroic "serum runs" to retrieve antitoxin.

SIBERIAN HUSKY

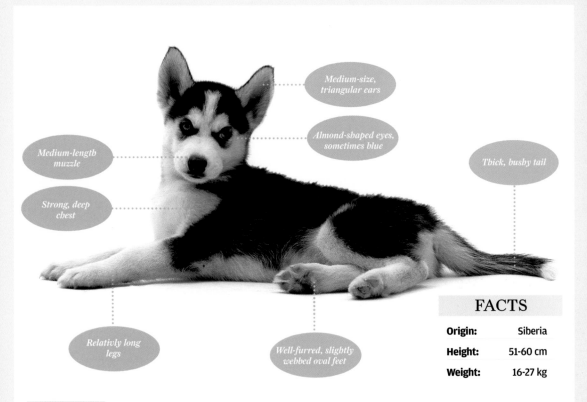

Medium-size, triangular ears

Almond-shaped eyes, sometimes blue

Thick, bushy tail

Medium-length muzzle

Strong, deep chest

Relativly long legs

Well-furred, slightly webbed oval feet

FACTS

Origin:	Siberia
Height:	51-60 cm
Weight:	16-27 kg

CHOICES

This is a starting breed in the Dachshund & Friends version. You can trade for it or unlock it in other Nintendogs versions.

 ## *Transportation with a tail*

Although smaller and lighter than some other breeds of sled dog, the Siberian husky is quick and athletic, and is a tireless worker. The dog was developed by the Chukchi people of northeast Asia as their only means of transportation. Brought to North America by fur traders to haul their sleds, the Siberian husky was used as a pack dog by Admiral Byrd during his historic Antarctic expedition in 1928. Although the Siberian husky is an excellent sled dog and a great companion, it makes a lousy watchdog because it barks little and loves everyone.

The toy poodle is known for superior intelligence and exceptional learning ability.

TOY POODLE

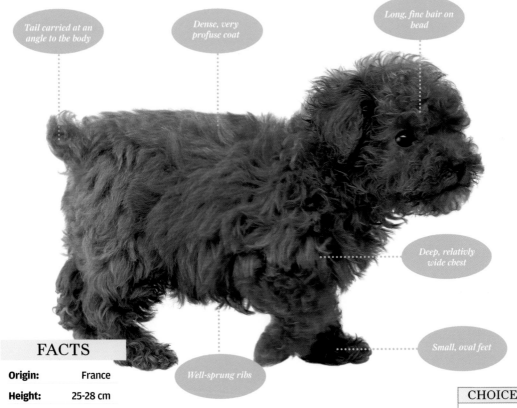

Tail carried at an angle to the body

Dense, very profuse coat

Long, fine hair on head

Deep, relatively wide chest

Small, oval feet

Well-sprung ribs

FACTS

Origin:	France
Height:	25-28 cm
Weight:	7 kg

 ## Viva la pooch!

If you've always dreamed of managing a supermodel, then the glamorous toy poodle is the pup for you. This elegant breed is known for sitting with royalty and dominating dog shows, but beauty does have its price—this high-maintenance but lovable diva needs to have its hair clipped every six weeks. Also known as a French poodle, the breed first became popular in France, where it was often used as a circus performer.

CHOICES

This is a starting breed in the Lab & Friends version. You can trade for it or unlock it in other Nintendogs versions.

YORKSHIRE TERRIER

The Yorkie became a fashionable pet in the late Victorian era.

Small, flat-topped head

Short, deep tan hair on ears

Short, level back

Rich, bright tan-colored hair on chest

Round feet

Straight limbs

FACTS

Origin:	Great Britain
Height:	23 cm
Weight:	3 kg

CHOICES

This is a starting breed in the Chihuahua & Friends and Dalmatian & Friends versions. You can trade for it or unlock it in other Nintendogs versions.

The teeny, tiny terrier

Named for its hometown in England, the Yorkshire terrier is one of the world's smallest canines. Rarely weighing more than seven pounds, this dinky dog seems to be completely oblivious to its small stature—it's always on the lookout for adventure and mischief. The Yorkshire terrier (or Yorkie) is known as a fashion dog today and is often seen under the arms of the rich and famous, but it was originally bred to chase rats out of the treacherous coal mines of England.

Time to Play

Now that you know the breeds, get to know the game.

PICK YOUR PUP

When you arrive at the Nintendogs kennel, you'll have your choice of a half-dozen different breeds, ranging in size, shape and temperament. With every color of the doggy rainbow to choose from, picking just one pup can be a daunting task. Luckily, the game provides detailed information about each dog's unique personality to help you find your perfect match.

THREE FOR THE ROAD

When you pick a breed, you will get three unique puppies to choose from, each with its own personality ranging from shy to spoiled, so be sure to read the fine print!

YOUR PUPPY PERSONALITY

Do you have beagle fever? Or are you more of a pug person? Each of the six initial breeds available at the Nintendogs kennel has specific traits—some are laid back and friendly, while others are more high-strung. If you are a first-time puppy parent, you may want to choose a low-maintenance breed like the Labrador retriever. If you're looking to make Best in Show, however, you might prefer a doggy diva like the toy poodle. Every breed is different, but if you do your research you'll find the ideal canine personality for you.

Home is where you hang your leash

When you first get home, your new doggy will be unsure of its surroundings. Make your pal feel welcome by lavishing it with affection and giving it a proper name. How about Pumpkin?

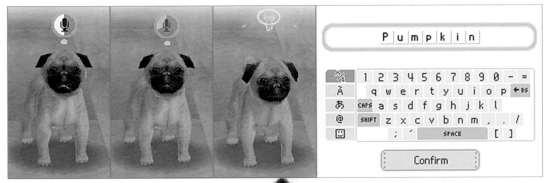

SHORT AND SWEET

Even though Little Lord Fancypants is a fine name for a dog, your young pup won't understand anything that complicated. Pick a one- or two-syllable name that's easy on the ears. Pickles? Good. Battleship Potemkin? Not so good. Once you've decided on the perfect name, it's time to teach it to your pup. When the gray microphone icon appears over the dog's head, say the name slowly and clearly. If your puppy hears you, the mic will turn red. If your puppy understands what you said, a lightbulb will then appear. Once you've said the name a few times, your puppy will learn its name and respond to it. Be sure to use its name often, because little puppies are forgetful.

THE BASICS

There's more to raising a dog than just choosing a cute name, of course—learning how to interact with your pet by navigating the various screens and menus is the first step toward being a grade-A puppy parent.

PUPPY SCREEN

This is where the magic happens. Petting, playing, bathing—it's all on the puppy screen.

1 Tap the arrow to return to the Home screen (see below).

2 Tap the box to view and use your supplies (page 84).

3 Tap the lightbulb to teach your puppy a new command (page 58).

HOME SCREEN

This screen is the hub for all of your Nintendogs activities. From here you can save your game, call your dog, monitor your supplies or head out of the house.

1 Save your game.

2 Supplies List—view and use your supplies (page 84).

3 Go Out—shows you places you can visit (page 55).

4 Tap this icon to whistle for your puppy.

5 Tap the small camera icon or touch the dog's face to zoom in on the dog.

6 Tap your dog's name or the ? icon to view the Dog Status screen (below).

DOG STATUS SCREEN

This page lets you know how your puppy is doing.

1 Tap the red arrow to return to the Home screen.

2 Trick List—view the tricks your puppy has learned (page 60).

3 Contest Results—see how well your pup has done in competitions (page 66).

MENU SCREEN

When you need to get out and do something, this is your starting place. From here you can access everything outside of your home as well as the Dog Status screen.

1 Tap the red arrow to return to the home screen (page 54).

2 The shopping icon takes you to the Shopping screen (see below).

3 Touch this to take your puppy for a walk (page 62).

4 Tap the wireless icon to set up Bark mode (page 95).

5 Tap the trophy to compete in three different contests (page 66).

6 The info icon opens the Info screen, which leads to the Trainer Info screen (see below), your Friend List and more.

7 The bottom of the screen displays a running tally of the money you have earned.

SHOPPING SCREEN

The shopping screen is like a Home Shopping Network for Nintendogs. With a touch of the stylus, you can buy basic pet supplies, sell unwanted items, buy another puppy, change your home decor or put your pup up in a fancy hotel.

1 Click here to go back home.

2 Pet Supply—you can buy basic pet supplies here.

3 Secondhand Shop—sell unwanted items for money.

4 Kennel—this is where you buy more puppies.

5 Interior Decorator—upgrade your home furnishings (page 70).

6 Dog Hotel—yes, you read that right: a place to park your pups.

TRAINER INFO SCREEN

This screen shows your name, birthday, Trainer Points and comments, plus a list of all your puppies. It also serves as a calling card that other owners can see when you're using Bark mode.

PUPPY CARE

Wash, brush, feed and provide water—these are the four basic things you need to do every day to keep your puppy happy. If you forget to take care of these important tasks on a daily basis, your pup will feel neglected and may even run away. Check the Dog Status screen to make sure your puppy has all of its basic needs met.

TOO MANY CHOICES?

Eventually you will have three types of food choices: dry, natural and canned. The dry kind is the cheapest, but your pup might resent eating from the bargain bin day in and day out, so treat it to the expensive food once in a while. Don't go overboard with the canned stuff, though, or you'll end up with a pudgy pooch!

RUB A DUB DUB

A clean dog is a happy dog, so be sure to wash and brush your pup at least once a day, especially before competitions, where your dog is judged on appearance as well as skill.

KEEP ON WALKING

Your energetic pup will go stir-crazy if it doesn't get outside once in a while. Take it for walks several times a day to burn off all that extra puppy energy—and so it can relieve itself!

SPEAK

When you first start speaking to your dog, it may give you some puzzled expressions. This is normal while you both get the hang of the training process. To be sure your puppy understands you, speak clearly with your mouth about six inches away from the microphone, and pick unique-sounding words—"shake" may sound too much like "sit" to your puppy, so try "handshake" instead. When your pup hears a word correctly, a little lightbulb will flash over its head. Good dog!

Say what?

Even the most keen-eared pup won't hear every new word you try to teach it. Red question marks will appear over your pup's head if it doesn't understand what you are saying, and blue question marks mean that a new command is too similar to one already learned. Keep trying—soon your little pupil will eagerly obey all your commands.

BASIC TRAINING

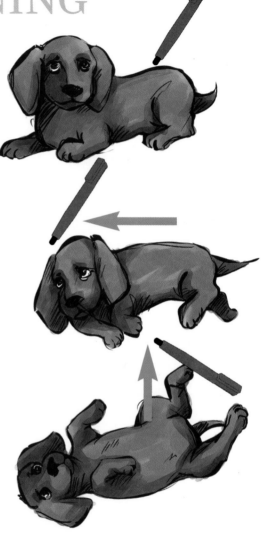

Y̲ou may not be able to teach an old dog new tricks, but your young puppy can learn plenty. "Sit" and "lie down" are the first couple of commands you will teach your pooch, but your puppy can learn dozens of different tricks. Here are a few to get you started.

SHAKE

With your puppy in the sitting position, gently lift its paw up and down. Be sure not to grab too forcefully, though, or your pup will let out a pitiful yelp!

ROLL OVER

While your dog is lying down, move the stylus over your puppy's back horizontally so it'll lie on its side, then slide the stylus up its furry belly to help your pup roll onto its back.

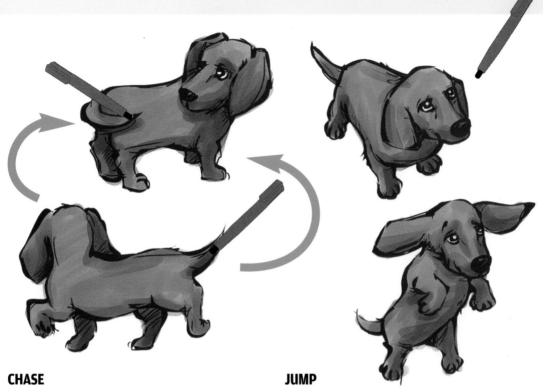

CHASE

There is nothing cuter than a puppy chasing its tail—*nothing*!
To teach your pup this trick, just grab onto its tail and wiggle it
until the dog notices—canine nature will do the rest.

JUMP

Does your dog like to shake its butt in your face? That means
it's ready to play. It also signals a good time to teach it how to
jump. Just tap in the air above its head and watch Fido leap.

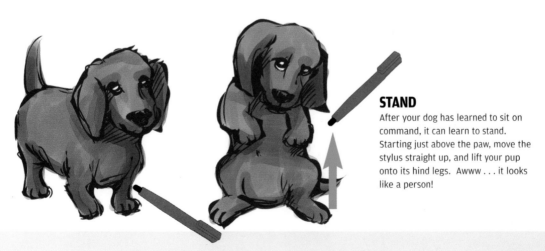

STAND

After your dog has learned to sit on
command, it can learn to stand.
Starting just above the paw, move the
stylus straight up, and lift your pup
onto its hind legs. Awww . . . it looks
like a person!

WALKING YOUR DOG

Are you getting cabin fever? Try stretching your legs with a walk around town. Your puppy will be a little squirrely on its first few outings as both of you learn the ropes, but soon your dog will practically walk itself.

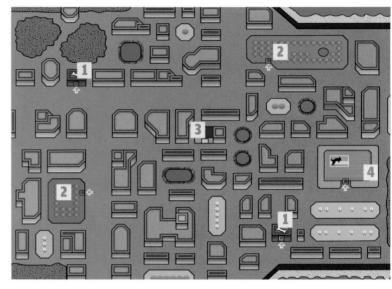

MAP SCREEN

This is a bird's-eye view of your entire town. It shows all the important places you'll want to visit with your dog. You won't be able to go very far at first, but once your pup builds up some stamina, you'll be able to explore more areas.

1 Discount shops—your one-stop puppy-supply shop.

2 Parks—great places to exercise and train for disc competitions.

3 Home—you will always start and end here.

4 Gymnasium—here you can train your puppy for agility competitions.

CHANCE GIFTS

When you are tooling around town with your pup, you might come across gifts sitting in the road but not marked on the map. Give a tug on the leash to have your pup retrieve them. Act fast—if you pass by a gift without picking it up, it'll be gone for good!

THE PARK

There are two parks on the map. One will have other dogs playing in it (it will have doggy icons on the map), while the other will be empty. If you'd like your pup to have some social time with other dogs, visit the occupied park. If you want to train your pup for flying-disc competitions, however, you'll want to visit the vacant park.

CLEAN UP YOUR MESS

Uh-oh! If poochie stops for a poo on the sidewalk, be sure to clean it up, or else you'll hear about it from your neighbors.

Practice makes perfect

Before you compete in an agility trial, take a walk to the gymnasium and try out all the different types of obstacles. Your pup will need plenty of coaching the first time through, but after a few runs, it'll be cruising through the course like a pro.

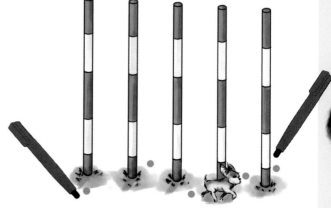

BAR JUMP

While your pup is in full gallop, tap the center of the bar. The faster your dog is running, the farther it will jump, which will impress the judges and earn you an "excellent" rating.

WEAVE POLES

Quickly tap out a weaving pattern for your pup to follow through the poles. Don't bump the poles, or you'll lose points.

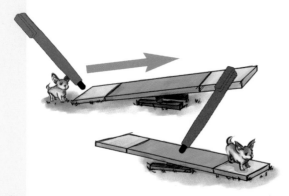

SEESAW

Draw a path across the seesaw. When your pup reaches the end, tap the middle of the seesaw to have your dog stop. Wait until the seesaw touches the ground before continuing, or your pup will fall off and you'll fail the test.

OPEN TUNNEL

Tap at the entrance to the tunnel. Once your puppy enters, drag the stylus through the tunnel, all the way to the end. Take it slow the first time, or your young pup might get stuck in the tunnel. If this happens, tap a path for your dog to follow out.

GARBAGE IN, GARBAGE OUT

When you take your hound for a walk, it'll stop and eat garbage off the sidewalk. Blech! To avoid this unpleasantness, tug on the leash.

Tyrone:
If you want to earn high scores in contests, you have to keep your dog sharp. That means constant training!

STRANGERS IN THE NIGHT

While you and your pup are out cruising the neighborhood, you might bump into another dog taking its human for a stroll. While the other trainer gives you helpful pup-raising tips, your dogs will get to know each other in the way that dogs do: by sniffing each other's rear!

COMPETITIONS

There are three main competition types: obedience, disc and agility. You will face off against other dog owners for cash prizes. Competitions are your main source of income, so it's important you learn how to master them.

OBEDIENCE COMPETITIONS

An obedience competition consists of timed rounds in which you and your puppy perform specific tricks. After a few games of Simon Says, your pup gets to freestyle—wow the judges with as many tricks as you can in 20 seconds.

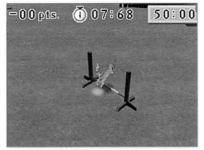

AGILITY COMPETITIONS

There are five different courses, each one increasingly difficult with new and more-challenging obstacles. Your loyal pal must clear all the obstacles in the correct order to complete the course. Be sure to get plenty of practice at the gymnasium before each competition to see what new challenges have appeared.

DISC COMPETITIONS

Start off simple and try to get your pup to go farther with each toss. Pay attention to the direction your dog is looking, and throw in that direction. Remember—longer throws mean more points, but only if your dog can make the catch.

SHOPS

There are six different shops in your town. You can access five of them—the pet supply store, secondhand shop, kennel, interior decorator (page 70) and dog hotel—from the Shopping screen (page 55), but you must walk to the discount shop (page 62). Even two different locations of the same store type will carry unique items, so visit them all.

Pet Supply

PET SUPPLY

The pet-supply shop carries standard items such as food, water, shampoo, brushes and a few accessories—all the basic needs for your special furry friend. As you earn money from competitions, you'll unlock more items.

Secondhand Shop

SECONDHAND SHOP

You can sell any oddball "presents" your pooch picks up on your walks here. Empty juice bottle, anyone?

DOG HOTEL

If you're going to be out of town or otherwise engaged, don't neglect your doggy. Instead, send it to the swankiest place in town: the dog hotel. Let the experts pamper your pooch with the finest canine accommodations money can buy. The dog hotel can hold up to five of your pups at a time, so send the whole family!

Dog Hotel

KENNEL

Does your best friend look a little down? Maybe it needs a playmate. The kennel is a fully licensed puppy provider with a large selection of purebred dogs in several different colors. If you don't see the color you want, exit the screen for the breed, then reenter it—there will be three new puppies of the breed to choose from.

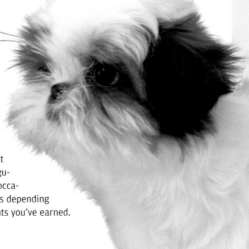

Kennel

Which dog would you like?

Siberian Husky
Originally bred in Russia, the husky recalls its ancestor, the wolf. Its trademarks are power and stamina.

$115,265.51

DISCOUNT SHOP

There are two discount shops in your town. They carry basic puppy items at a lower price than the regular supply shop, and will occasionaly carry special items depending on how many trainer points you've earned.

Discount Shop

Time for a new doghouse

After you've won all of the competitions, you may be wondering what to do with all of your newly acquired wealth. How about buying a new house? There are eight home upgrades available at the interior decorator's shop, ranging from common condo to cuckoo-crazy!

Interior Decorator

DESIGNER CONDO—$500

A slight upgrade over your starter home, this modern condo offers all the bare neccessities at a rock-bottom price.

URBAN LIVING—$1,500

A swanky bachelor pad for the swingin' type. It offers an urban oasis of slick, city style. If you like to live the high life, this place is for you.

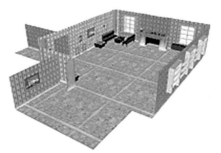

EARLY AMERICAN—$1,000

Movin' on up—a full-sized, classic American house, complete with a fireplace and furnishings for your growing family (and income).

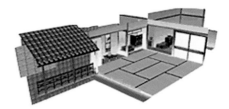

TATAMI ROOM—$5,000

The ultimate in Asian elegance, the tatami room is the perfect place for quiet meditation.

NORTHERN EUROPEAN—$5,000

You can finally stop drooling over those Swedish furniture catalogs and just buy the whole store. The finest in Scandinavian simplicity.

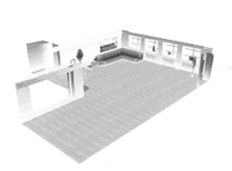

DESKTOP—$20,000

Do you sometimes wish you could bring your dog to work with you? Well, your dreams have been answered. Now you can see Spot run all over your carefully crafted spreadsheets.

SEASIDE—$50,000

Now this is living! You and your pooch posse can lounge in style at your new seaside crib. Donald Trump, eat your heart out!

OUTER SPACE—$100,000

What do you get the show dog who has everything? How about your very own private space station. Just cross your fingers that engineers have figured out the "zero-gravity doggy poo" problem before you move in.

Canine Q & A

Is your puppy acting strangely? Gain some insight into your pup's mind straight from the experts.

PUPPY PROBLEMS

Does Spot stare at you blankly when you speak to him? Does Fifi leap up when you want her to lie down? The following pages answer many of the questions you might have about your Nintendog (but were afraid to ask).

Q: *What are Trainer Points?*

A: Trainer Points are a way of measuring your relationship with your puppy. The more time you spend training and playing with your pup, the more points you'll earn. You can also boost your Trainer Points by making sure your dog is groomed, fed and given water on a regular basis. As your bond with your pup grows, your point total will grow as well, unlocking special items and even rare dog breeds.

Q: *How do I earn money?*

A: There are a couple of ways to earn money in Nintendogs. The big money lies in the competitions, where you can earn thousands of dollars a day once you reach the advanced class. If you need money in a pinch, you can always sell items at the secondhand shop, but you won't make much—most items sell for ten dollars or less.

Q: *Why is my puppy going nuts?*

A: If your puppy is running around like his tail is on fire when you're trying to teach him a new trick, he's probably suffering from training overload. A tiny puppy brain can learn only so much in a day. Try taking your little buddy out for a walk—when you get back, he may be ready for more lessons.

QUICK TIP

Your puppy can learn three tricks a day. Plan carefully, and don't exhaust your pooch!

Q: *Why does my puppy whine and nip at me when I touch her?*

A: If your dog gets mad at you or yelps when you pet her, that's dog talk for "bad touch!" Puppies dislike being petted on certain parts of their bodies. The ears and paws are the most common no-no spots. The amount of pressure and how fast you pet the dog can be factors, as well.

A slow rub across your puppy's head will usually make her sparkle with delight. Pay close attention—your puppy will tell you exactly how she likes to be handled.

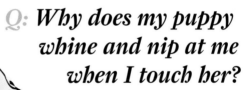

Q: *How do I know which puppy is right for me?*

A:　When you first visit the kennel, you may have a hard time choosing from the dozens of adorable pups available. If you look closely, though, you'll find that each dog has a unique personality. Zoom in on each of the pups to get a good look at how it gets along with its kennel mates. After you choose one of the six initial breeds, you'll be able to read more about each of the pups' different temperaments, from easygoing to over-bearing. If, after examining all the dogs, you still haven't found your soul mate, take a break and come back later—different dogs will be available each time you visit.

Q: *How often should I wash and brush my dog?*

A: Wash and brush your dog at least once a day. If you skip a few days, your pup will get fleas (not to mention low self-esteem.) Be sure to use the right shampoo and brush for your dog's hair type—if you don't know your dog's hair type, you can view the Dog Status screen (page 54) to find out.

Q: *Where can I score that sweet Mario dog hat?*

A: Most of the accessories are available only as found gifts, and the best found gifts (like the Mario hat) are usually located at the farthest points on the map. When you first get your puppy, it can travel only a few blocks, but if you go for walks every day, your dog will build up stamina and you'll soon be going on long-distance gift-hunting expeditions together.

Q: *My puppy is great at disc competitions, but not so good in the agility trials—what should I do?*

A: Three words: practice, practice, practice. Your puppy probably wasn't very good at catching discs when it first started either, but with practice it improved enough to compete. The more practice your pup gets in any competition, the better it will do. Head over to the Agility Training Center (page 64) and run through the course several times until your little canine athlete can clear all the obstacles with ease.

Q: *How can I get my pups to stop fighting?*

A: Music soothes the savage beast, and it will pacify your pup as well. If your doggy house-
mates are constantly nipping at each other, try putting on a relaxing record to calm
them down. You can find several different types of records in gift boxes around town—some
are well-suited for group exercise, some for getting your puppies' attention and even some for
helping them fall asleep. Experiment with a variety of different tunes to find out which ones
your pups prefer.

Q: *My pup has mastered all the basics—are there some advanced tricks I can teach it?*

A: There are dozens of "secret" moves you can teach your dog. One of the coolest is the backflip. Start by having your dog sit. From the sitting position, tell him to jump. If your command is successful, your pooch will leap up and perform a perfect backward flip. You might have an Olympic gymnast on your hands!

Q: *How do I give presents to other dog owners?*

A: Whether you're introducing yourself to other dog owners or trading items with friends, gift-giving is one of the best features in Nintendogs. When you first enter Bark mode, you'll be asked if you'd like to bring a gift. Select the item you'd like to give away—your pup will do the rest. Make sure you're really willing to part with your gift—once you give away that prized rainbow wig, it'll be gone for good.

Q: *My puppy sits when I want it to shake—what gives?*

A: Your pup's ears aren't perfect. If you've used words that sound too similar, your dog might be confused. Check the trick list on the Dog Status screen to see if any of the commands start with the same letter, like "sit" and "shake." Delete one of the moves and retrain your pup using a different term, such as "handshake" instead of "shake."

Pup Supplies

More dog stuff than you can shake a stick at!

POOCH PRODUCTS

Who knew puppies needed so much stuff? Luckily, your friendly neighborhood pet shop has everything your dog could ever want . . . and then some!

CARE These are the bare necessities for keeping your pup happy and healthy. You can purchase these items at the pet-supply store or the discount shop.

Dog Biscuits
PURCHASE PRICE:
$.30
SELLING PRICE:
$.10

Nothing says "good dog!" like old-fashioned dog biscuits.

Jerky Treats
PURCHASE PRICE:
$.50
SELLING PRICE:
$.20

Your puppy will love these meatlike chewy treats—and you might too!

Water Bottle
PURCHASE PRICE:
$.60
SELLING PRICE:
$.20

Apparently there's no running water at your place, so doggy gets to drink mountain-fresh mineral water.

Milk Carton
PURCHASE PRICE:
$1.00
SELLING PRICE:
$.40

Milk is a special treat for your lactose-tolerant pup. It does a doggy body good!

Dry Food
PURCHASE PRICE:
$1.50
SELLING PRICE:
$.60

Economy-line dog food is half the price (and half the flavor) of that fancy canned type.

Dog Food Can
PURCHASE PRICE:
$3.00
SELLING PRICE:
$1.20

If you really love your dog, you'll treat him to some tasty canned food once in a while.

Natural Dog Food
PURCHASE PRICE:
$5.00
SELLING PRICE:
$2.00

When canned food just isn't good enough for your pup, try the earth-friendly Natural Dog Food.

Short-Hair Shampoo
PURCHASE PRICE:
$1.30
SELLING PRICE:
$.50

Keep your short-haired puppy (and your house) flea-free with this doggy shampoo.

Long-Hair Shampoo
PURCHASE PRICE:
$1.80
SELLING PRICE:
$.70

Use a special shampoo for your long-haired pup.

Rubber Brush
PURCHASE PRICE:
$30.00
SELLING PRICE:
$12.00

Make your short-haired dog sparkle with this rubber hair brush.

Wire Brush
PURCHASE PRICE:
$40.00
SELLING PRICE:
$16.00

When rubber just won't do, try this deluxe wire hair brush for your lovely, Rapunzel-tressed dog.

CHEW TOYS

These playthings help strengthen your young pup's teeth and relieve stress. You'll come across these (and the rest of the items listed in this book) on your walks, and you'll even see some of the items in stores.

White Rubber Bone

PURCHASE PRICE: VARIES

SELLING PRICE: $1.60

De-stress your pup with a nice, rubber chew toy. Perfect for playing fetch.

Red Rubber Bone

PURCHASE PRICE: VARIES

SELLING PRICE: $1.60

This is just like the white rubber bone, but in bright and cheerful red.

Blue Rubber Bone

PURCHASE PRICE: VARIES

SELLING PRICE: $1.60

Your playful pup will enjoy a blue chew.

Bicolor Rubber Bone

PURCHASE PRICE: VARIES

SELLING PRICE: $1.60

Everyone's favorite chew toy is back, but this time it's striped.

Tennis Ball

PURCHASE PRICE: VARIES

SELLING PRICE: $2.00

Your dog will love chasing this classic yellow tennis ball around the house or at the park.

Bark Ball

SELLING PRICE: $3.00

If your doggy likes noise and toys, he'll go bonkers over the amazing Bark Ball.

Rubber Mushroom

SELLING PRICE: $4.00

Buy your pup a squeaky shroom that makes a variety of noises when chewed or thrown.

Soccer Ball

SELLING PRICE: $6.00

Your favorite soccer team hasn't won a game in two years—maybe your dog can help.

? Block

SELLING PRICE: $6.00

Bewilder and amuse your puppy with the mysterious ? Block.

Dice Cushion

SELLING PRICE: $5.00

If you think dogs playing poker is funny, imagine the hilarity of puppies playing D&D!

Terry Cloth Cube

SELLING PRICE: $4.00

Is your puppy teething? Let him sink his fangs into this colorful, plush cube.

DISCS

A wide variety of colorful, flying toys will help your pup in disc competitions.

Red Flying Disc
PURCHASE PRICE:
$6.00
SELLING PRICE:
$2.40

The classic red flying disc is perfect for competitions.

Blue Flying Disc
PURCHASE PRICE:
$6.00
SELLING PRICE:
$2.40

The classic flying disc is now available in blue.

Yellow Flying Disc
PURCHASE PRICE:
VARIES
SELLING PRICE:
$2.40

There's also a bright yellow version of the flying disc.

Blue Camo Disc
SELLING PRICE:
$4.00

The blue camo disc is great for playing catch in the Arctic snow!

Khaki Camo Disc
SELLING PRICE:
$4.00

Is your dog a military hound? Then this khaki camo disc is for you.

Yellow Sponsor Disc
PURCHASE PRICE:
VARIES
SELLING PRICE:
$5.00

Your pal can play with the official yellow flying disc of the Nintendogs league.

Green Sponsor Disc
PURCHASE PRICE:
VARIES
SELLING PRICE:
$5.00

This is the official *green* flying disc of the Nintendogs league.

Pink Aerodisc
SELLING PRICE:
$6.00

This pink aerodisc gets extra air—and extra style points.

White Aerodisc
SELLING PRICE:
$6.00

This is eerily similar to the pink aerodisc, only white.

Shower Cap
SELLING PRICE:
$2.00

It may look like an ordinary shower cap, but it's actually a waterproof flying toy.

Broken Clock
SELLING PRICE:
$2.00

It may no longer tell time, but this broken clock makes a great dog toy.

Life Ring
SELLING PRICE:
$2.00

Not only can this life ring save lives, but it makes a good toy for playing catch with your dog.

Dartboard
SELLING PRICE:
$10.00

This dartboard lost its darts, but it still makes a great flying disc.

Pizza Disc
SELLING PRICE:
$10.00

Did someone order a stale pizza? It may not taste good, but your dog will love chasing this flying food.

UFO
SELLING PRICE:
$10.00

Extraterrestrial transportation or just a shiny new toy for your dog? You make the call.

OTHER TOYS

Here's an assortment of weird and wacky toys for your furry buddy.

Balloon
PURCHASE PRICE:
$.30
SELLING PRICE:
$.10

This red balloon will be your pup's favorite toy—until it pops!

Bubble Blower
SELLING PRICE:
$1.00

Blow through this magic wand and watch your dog chase the bubbles.

Pull Rope
PURCHASE PRICE:
$8.00
SELLING PRICE:
$3.20

Now you and your pup can play tug-of-war with this extrastrong pull rope.

Jump Rope
PURCHASE PRICE:
$10.00
SELLING PRICE:
$4.00

This jump rope is a perfect toy for your pups to share during playtime.

Windup Toy
PURCHASE PRICE:
$30.00
SELLING PRICE:
$12.00

Wind up this mechanical man and watch your dogs chase him across the room.

Talking Bird
PURCHASE PRICE:
$40.00
SELLING PRICE:
$16.00

Be careful when you speak around this talking bird—it likes to repeat what you say.

Mario Kart
SELLING PRICE:
$100.00

Now you can play Mario Kart on your living-room floor with this radio-controlled toy.

Bowser Kart
SELLING PRICE:
$100.00

This radio-controlled car features Mario's enemy, Bowser, at the wheel.

Peach Kart
SELLING PRICE:
$100.00

Mario's sweetheart, Princess Peach, is featured in this speedy radio-controlled kart.

RC Helicopter
SELLING PRICE:
$200.00

Watch your head! This radio-controlled helicopter can fly indoors or outside.

Combat Copter
SELLING PRICE:
$300.00

If you love the smell of napalm in the morning, then this radio-controlled copter is a must-have.

COLLARS

Every dog should have a collar. There are dozens to choose from, ranging from plain to punk-rock.

Red Leather Collar
PURCHASE PRICE:
$10.00
SELLING PRICE:
$4.00

This is a classic red collar for your pooch.

Black Leather Collar
PURCHASE PRICE:
$10.00
SELLING PRICE:
$4.00

Your little bruiser will love a tough-looking black leather collar.

Purple Leather Collar
PURCHASE PRICE:
VARIES
SELLING PRICE:
$4.00

What pup wouldn't be stunning in a pretty purple collar?

Green Leather Collar
PURCHASE PRICE:
VARIES
SELLING PRICE:
$4.00

Celebrate St. Patrick's Day in style with this green leather dog collar.

Pumpkin Leather Collar
PURCHASE PRICE:
VARIES
SELLING PRICE:
$4.00

Although this collar is pumpkin-colored, it still tastes like leather.

Blue Leather Collar
PURCHASE PRICE:
VARIES
SELLING PRICE:
$4.00

A bright-blue dog collar will suit your bright new pup.

Dot Collar
SELLING PRICE:
$10.00

A colorful, polka-dot pooch collar gives your friend panache.

Camo Collar
SELLING PRICE:
$10.00

A camo collar is ideal for your combat canine.

Rainbow Collar
SELLING PRICE:
$10.00

A rainbow collar looks good on dogs of every color.

Denim Collar
SELLING PRICE:
$10.00

Denim is the collar of choice for farm dogs everywhere.

Platinum Collar
SELLING PRICE:
$10.00

A sleek and stylish collar complements a modern dog.

Woven Collar
SELLING PRICE:
$10.00

Consider a rustic, hand-woven collar for the earthy type.

Lucky Collar
SELLING PRICE:
$10.00

Even lucky dogs need a little help sometimes, and this special gem will do the trick.

Flower Collar
SELLING PRICE:
$10.00

Your pup princess will go gaga over this flower-powered collar.

Spiked Collar
SELLING PRICE:
$10.00

You can't have a punk-rock pooch without a punk-rock collar.

Japanese Print Collar
SELLING PRICE:
$10.00

This beautiful collar is decorated with a Japanese motif.

Rhinestone Collar
SELLING PRICE:
$10.00

This sparkling, jewel-encrusted collar is a must for any doggy diva.

Pearl Necklace
SELLING PRICE:
$10.00

Give the ultimate gift to the elegant lady pup in your life.

RIBBONS

There's nothing like a fancy ribbon to top off a beautiful pup. You can find ribbons in an assortment of colors and designs.

Red Ribbon
PURCHASE PRICE:
$6.00
SELLING PRICE:
$2.40

A classic red ribbon makes a great adornment for your classy dog.

Yellow Ribbon
PURCHASE PRICE:
$6.00
SELLING PRICE:
$2.40

Tie a yellow ribbon 'round that little puppy of yours.

Checked Ribbon
SELLING PRICE:
$4.00

This checkered ribbon is very popular with the female pooches.

Striped Ribbon
SELLING PRICE:
$4.00

Buy a fancy green topper for your dapper pup.

Red Polka-Dot Ribbon
SELLING PRICE:
$7.00

A festive polka-dot design is just right for a fancy dog.

Blue Polka-Dot Ribbon
SELLING PRICE:
$7.00

A smart blue ribbon with polka-dots will look great on your natty pooch.

Tricolor Ribbon
SELLING PRICE:
$10.00

Put the red, white and blue on your patriotic pooch.

Purple Pearl Ribbon
SELLING PRICE:
$18.00

Treat your special pup to a gorgeous purple pearl ribbon.

Green Pearl Ribbon
SELLING PRICE:
$18.00

This green pearl ribbon is an ideal accessory for your dignified doggy.

FLOWERS

Spruce up your pooch with some beautiful flowers.

Rose
SELLING PRICE: $10.00

Buy a regal rose for your romantic pup.

Hibiscus Flower
SELLING PRICE: $10.00

An exotic flower will bring a touch of the tropics to your home.

Lily
SELLING PRICE: $10.00

This colorful lily will brighten up any home.

GLASSES

If you'd like to give your doggy a fashionable flair, fit him with some special specs.

Scholar Glasses
SELLING PRICE: $9.00

Instantly increase your pup's I.Q. with these brainy specs.

Business Glasses
SELLING PRICE: $12.00

A serious dog needs serious glasses.

Huge Sunglasses
SELLING PRICE: $15.00

Your dog will be ready to boogie the night away in these retro lenses.

Sport Sunglasses
SELLING PRICE: $19.00

Turn the cool meter up to 11 with these futuristic shades.

Party Glasses
SELLING PRICE: $7.00

Now your pup can keep an eye on *you* with these creepy "party" glasses.

3-D Glasses
SELLING PRICE: $9.00

Take fido on far-out adventures with these 3-D glasses.

Star Sunglasses
SELLING PRICE: $9.00

Funkify your pup with these superfly sunglasses.

HATS

Every dog loves a good hat. Have your pooch try one on for size.

Ten-Gallon Hat
SELLING PRICE:
$14.00

This hat is all the rage with canine cowboys.

Yellow Cap
SELLING PRICE:
$8.00

Take your dog out to the ball game with this stylish yellow cap.

Red & Blue Cap
SELLING PRICE:
$8.00

Your buddy will shine in a classic two-tone baseball cap.

Beret
SELLING PRICE:
$10.00

A beret is a must-have for your budding young artist.

Straw Hat
SELLING PRICE:
$9.00

If your dog likes to dig in the yard, he'll love this straw gardening hat.

Newsboy Hat
SELLING PRICE:
$16.00

This vintage hat will make your pup look like an old-time newsboy.

Red Hat
SELLING PRICE:
$20.00

This is the perfect hat for your little puppy plumber.

Green Hat
SELLING PRICE:
$20.00

This floppy green hat pays tribute to that *other* famous plumber.

Knit Hat
SELLING PRICE:
$10.00

A warm hat will keep your pup's ears warm during the winter.

Pirate Hat
SELLING PRICE:
$24.00

Argh! Feast your eyes on this fearsome hat, matey!

Tiara
SELLING PRICE:
$30.00

If you treat your pup like a princess, maybe it's time to dress her like one.

Crown
SELLING PRICE:
$30.00

Crown your dog "The King of Pupdom" with this royal headgear.

Rack of Deer Antlers
SELLING PRICE:
$30.00

With these antlers, your puppy will be ready to pull Santa's sled.

Graduation Cap
SELLING PRICE:
$18.00

Your dog will look like the top of his class with this graduation cap.

Party Hat
SELLING PRICE:
$10.00

Nothing says "party" like a dog with a birthday cake on its head.

Top Hat
SELLING PRICE:
$18.00

This top hat is ideal for both millionaire and magician pups.

Sombrero
SELLING PRICE:
$10.00

A big sombrero provides shade for your south-of-the-border doggy.

Viking Hat
SELLING PRICE:
$40.00

This Nordic headgear is designed for roaming the frozen fjords of viking country.

Santa's Hat
SELLING PRICE:
$18.00

Dress up doggy like one of Santa's little helpers with this holiday hat.

New Year Tiara
SELLING PRICE:
$12.00

Let your pup ring in the new year in style with this glimmering party tiara.

Fireman's Hat
SELLING PRICE:
$30.00

This hat can mean only one thing: dalmatians!

Rainbow Wig
SELLING PRICE:
$20.00

Your puppy will be ready to hit the dance floor in this psychedelic rainbow wig.

Lion's Mane
SELLING PRICE:
$20.00

Your pup will rule the urban jungle with this lion's mane.

CLOCKS

These colorful clocks replace the standard model that rests in the upper-right corner of your screen.

Marine Clock
SELLING PRICE:
$16.00

Silver Clock
SELLING PRICE:
$16.00

Wall Clock
SELLING PRICE:
$16.00

Clover Clock
SELLING PRICE:
$16.00

Smart Clock
SELLING PRICE:
$16.00

Marble Clock
SELLING PRICE:
$16.00

Cube Clock
SELLING PRICE:
$16.00

MUSIC

What's your puppy's favorite type of music? Try some of these records to find out.

Red Records
SELLING PRICE:
$5.00

Street Marker: This is a great exercise record for your pooch. **Growler:** This disc will get your pup all riled up! **Smilin' Dog:** This record plays a happy song for happy pups. **Friendly Whiff:** Social dogs will appreciate this record's tunes. **Chow:** Play some diner music for your doggy.

Blue Records
SELLING PRICE:
$9.00

Surprise: Play a prank on your pup with this startling record. **Naptime:** This disc makes your puppy sleepy. **Colonel Bogey:** Get your dog marching with this military tune. **Toreador:** Your dog will love this stirring Bizet opera piece. **Flower Waltz:** This classical piece by Tchaikovsky may stir your pup to dance. **Nintendogs:** Your pups will "sing" along with this one.

Green Records
SELLING PRICE:
$10.00

Waves: Some pups will revel in this new-age relaxation record. **Modest Decor:** This record plays a tune for indoor activity. **Shredded Fur:** This is a special remix LP. **Giant Socks:** This one might make your pups yawn.

Keyboard
PURCHASE PRICE:
$200.00
SELLING PRICE:
$80.00

Your pups will happily sing along in key while you play this pocket-sized piano.

Dog's Theme Box
SELLING PRICE:
$6.00

Your dog deserves its very own theme music.

Mario's Theme Box
SELLING PRICE:
$6.00

This box plays the famous plumber's theme song.

Puppy's Theme Box
SELLING PRICE:
$6.00

A classic Chopin tune plays on this music box.

Dictionary Box
SELLING PRICE:
$6.00

This music box plays your personal greeting for your pet.

White Record
FREE

This record lets you record a brief message that other trainers will hear when you are in Bark mode.

Some items are so wacky they defy categorization!

Stick
SELLING PRICE:
$.50

Tissue Box
SELLING PRICE:
$1.00

Dog Photo
SELLING PRICE:
$2.00

Disposable Camera
SELLING PRICE:
$2.40

Juice Bottle
SELLING PRICE:
$.80

Leather Shoe
SELLING PRICE:
$6.00

Pump
SELLING PRICE:
$6.00

High Heel
SELLING PRICE:
$6.00

Black Boot
SELLING PRICE:
$9.00

White Boot
SELLING PRICE:
$9.00

Lisa Doll
SELLING PRICE:
$30.00

Stuffed Dog
SELLING PRICE:
$50.00

Stuffed Bear
SELLING PRICE:
$60.00

Moai Statue
SELLING PRICE:
$100.00

Globe
SELLING PRICE:
$30.00

Space Shuttle
SELLING PRICE:
$50.00

Meteorite
SELLING PRICE:
$150.00

Weird Alien
SELLING PRICE:
$600.00

Promise Ring
SELLING PRICE:
$1,000.00

Gold Bar
SELLING PRICE:
$2,000.00

Piggy Bank
SELLING PRICE:
$2.00

Vase
SELLING PRICE:
$20.00

Fine Vase
SELLING PRICE:
$100.00

Very Fine Vase
SELLING PRICE:
$200.00

Jack Russell Book
SELLING PRICE:
$3.60

Bark Mode

*Have a puppy playdate with other trainers
via your wireless connection.*

BARK MODE

Does your puppy need a pal? Bark mode lets you search for other Nintendogs owners in your area (up to 65 feet away). You can exchange trainer info, trade items and even unlock additional breeds in your kennel. It's time to socialize!

PUPPY PLAYMATES

When you meet someone in Bark mode, your puppies will play with each other. The pup you meet will even stick around for a while after its owner has left.

TAKE A GIFT

When you go out, have your puppy bring a gift for any owner you might bump into. If you're lucky, the other owner will have a gift for you, as well.

FRIEND LIST

Any time you meet a dog owner in Bark mode, that person's trainer info will be saved to your Friend List automatically. You can save up to 50 contacts on the list.

HOOK UP

Is your DS barking at you? That means your puppy has met a new friend. If your system is in Bark mode, it will continue to look for new contacts even when your DS is closed.